The mature motorist's driving coach

Rick Appleton

Copyright © 2014 Rick Appleton

All rights reserved, including the right to reproduce this book, or portions thereof in any form. No part of this text may be reproduced, transmitted, downloaded, decompiled, reverse engineered, or stored, in any form or introduced into any information storage and retrieval system, in any form or by any means, whether electronic or mechanical without the express written permission of the author.

ISBN: 978-1-326-09711-0

INDEX

Ignition	1
The Ageing Process	5
Motivation	8
'Roadcraft'	12
'The Highway Code'	15
Principles	16
Skills	19
Steering	22
Braking	25
Gears and Throttle	28
Unconscious Competence	32
Strategies	33
'I' Information	34
'P' Position	39
'S' 'G' Speed and gear	47
More on speed	50
'A' Acceleration Sense	53
Driving Environments	58
Adverse Conditions	68
Mindset	72
Appendix	76

Ignition

Congratulations! You have just taken what could be one of the most important steps in your life, a step which could have literally life-changing consequences for you!

What on earth am I talking about?

All you've done is pick up a book and started reading.   Correct.

A small and possibly insignificant act in your busy life but now you cannot escape from making a decision;

are you going to acknowledge the fact that your driving skills are capable of improvement or are you going to continue in the belief that the quality of your driving is beyond reproach?

I don't say that your driving isn't excellent – only that I know without the smallest shadow of doubt that it is capable of becoming even better.

Every one of us can be a better driver.
Better today than we were yesterday and
better tomorrow than we are today!

The first requirement is a change in our attitude and in our approach. There are two attributes in this life where the human race seems to be almost universally blinkered; nearly everybody is convinced that they have a well developed sense of humour and nearly everybody believes that they are good drivers.   When did you last hear anybody contradicting either of these?   Well I can't do anything about your sense of humour but I am confident that your driving competence

can definitely be improved – if you're prepared to be teachable and prepared to put in some effort.
As I have already said it starts with a change of attitude.
Still reading?   Excellent!   Things are definitely looking promising! I guess that means that you accept that the above statement in bold type could actually refer to you and you would like to give it a try.

This book is entitled 'The Mature Motorist's Driving Coach'
What do I mean by a Mature Motorist?
When we start to drive we take lessons from a driving instructor and then take a driving test to establish whether we can be regarded as safe to be let loose on the roads.

This is the <u>starting-point</u> at which we begin to gain experience.

Thereafter the majority of us are to a large extent self taught with additional input from observing other people who are also self taught. The amount of practice and experience we obtain is extremely variable but after a period of time we become confident and more competent until driving becomes 'second nature' and can be and frequently is, carried out with very little conscious thought.

A mature driver is someone who has reached this point but recognises that familiarity can result in a tendency to a reduction in concentration levels which needs conscious effort to be avoided.
The word mature also carries an implication of age, but ability isn't determined by our chronological age or the number of years of our driving experience.   Some individuals are 'old' at 50 whilst others remain comparatively 'young' in their 90s. What is of paramount importance is the recognition that although long experience has its benefits these may be reduced or even negated by the inevitable onset of physical deterioration. Consequently when the onset of this

physical deterioration is recognised or suspected it inescapably enters the equation of driving competence.

It seems to me therefore that there are two groups of readers who would be happy to regard themselves as a 'Mature Motorist;

    a) Experienced drivers at any age;

    b) Experienced drivers who are coming to recognise that they 'are not as young as they used to be' and are wondering if this could create problems in the future.

These two groups can both benefit from this book but in slightly different ways.

Before expanding on this difference, a word about the word 'coach'. I deliberately avoid using the terms 'instructor or 'teacher' which it would be inappropriate to apply to a mature person.   It's rather like the difference between school, where pupils are taught and university, where students are tutored to take advantage of available learning resources but are ultimately responsible for themselves.

So first; group a).

If you are serious about wanting to improve your driving I suggest that you consider joining a local group of either the Institute of Advanced Motorists (IAM) or the Royal Society for the Prevention of Accidents (RoSPA) with the intention of ultimately taking the advanced motorist's driving test.   There you will receive coaching, in your own car at your own convenience in your own time, sufficient to prepare you for the test for however long that may prove to be. You will have a personal coach to provide all the help you need. However you may find the advice in this book an additional benefit.

Now, Group b)

You are concerned to ensure that your driving does not deteriorate as a consequence of the ageing process. You are prepared to put in some time and effort to this end but at this moment do not have any aspirations to take an advanced driving test.

This book is designed for you.

The ageing Process

Before getting down to the nitty gritty of the interesting topic of improving driving performance it is necessary to briefly address the subject of those' frailties of the flesh'. Not to beat about the bush we're none of us as young as we used to be and we need to make sure that the effects of physical changes on driving are minimised. Sooner or later, if we are one of the fortunate long lifers, the time will come when we realise that our driving days are over but thank goodness that day can be postponed as a result of our own personal effort. This booklet will help you to do this.

Eyesight.

The Law requires the ability to read a number plate at a distance of 20 meters, if necessary wearing your own prescribed glasses.
A useful and easy way of checking this is to log on to the website **www.vutest.com/seedrive.**   This is a number plate simulator which changes every 10 seconds.
 N.B you have to follow instructions about the viewing distance from the screen related to your screen size.

If you have any doubt whatsoever about your vision you should consult an optician.

Hearing

Hearing can be very important - for instance approaching a blind junction on a country road. In these circumstances it may help to open both car windows.
If hearing is diminished I would advise turning the radio off in heavy traffic.

Mobility

It is essential to be very honest with yourself if there is any doubt about full physical control and to realise that an awful lot of benefit may result from seat and steering wheel adjustments. The DVLA places the responsibility for fitness to drive on the individual driver but
   if there is any doubt at all you should consult your doctor.

Fatigue

In the past you may have been able to drive for prolonged periods without tiring significantly but as time goes by this ability lessens. On long journeys make a point to
   have a break or change of driver every 2 hours

This is a useful rule of thumb. Be particularly alert to
   **not allowing your attention to slip during
   the last few miles from your destination.**

This is the time when concentration slackens as tiredness sets in. Statistically the majority of collisions occur within a few miles of home.

Night driving.

Night driving always increases the level of stress particularly on motorways and in bad weather.
Adjust your planning to reduce night driving to a minimum.

Motivation

The fact that you're reading this book at all is an indication that you recognise that your driving could possibly be improved. However to achieve this is going to involve quite a lot of effort over a prolonged period of time and a considerable amount of determination.

Deeply ingrained habits can't be changed just by recognising them and making a decision on a wave of enthusiasm.

In order to maintain momentum it is necessary to be suitably motivated.

First and foremost driving should be a pleasure.

If it is becoming stressful it may not be entirely due to a change in road conditions. A much more likely reason is that your confidence level is beginning to slip. The simple way to increase confidence is to take active steps to refurbish old skills and acquire new ones. Although changing deeply established habits can at first seem difficult and of questionable benefit, I promise you that with perseverance your driving experiences will become much more satisfying and enjoyable.

Secondly, but probably of far more importance, is the question of SAFETY.
Road accident statistics do not make pleasant reading and it is very easy to think that they only apply to other people.
Every day in this country, on average, 5 people are killed in motoring incidents and another 60 have life changing injuries.
The very word accident is a misnomer;

in around 95% of cases the 'accident' could have been prevented if someone had done something different.

The aviation industry refers to this as 'pilot error.'

It is actually statistically true that senior citizens have a lower proportion of collisions than younger people, but it is also statistically true that the resulting injuries are far more severe.
I hope that no one reading this book will have to look back in the future and say "if only I'd taken more notice".
It's your life we're talking about and possibly other people's lives as well.   There's an old saying "if something is worth doing it's worth doing well".   It certainly applies to driving.

Aims and ambitions

How do we judge our driving proficiency?
What sort of level should we be aiming at?
Are we 'average'?
What is average anyway?
Should we aim to be 'above average'?

As with the assessment of any characteristic or skill, driving ability can be represented by a 'bell curve,' so called because of its shape.

The "bell" distribution curve

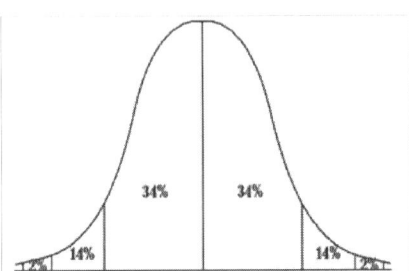

Along the horizontal axis is performance from zero on the left to perfection on the right. The vertical axis represents the number of people at each of these stages.

There are a few really bad drivers represented at the left hand end, who really shouldn't be on the roads at all. It is sobering to think that with a licensed population of 45 million drivers in the UK at least one million or so (a conservative 2%) represent a tangible danger.

All the more reason for the rest of us to be as vigilant as possible to guard against their unpredicted actions.

The majority of drivers fall in the middle range (average to good), and a comparatively small number are really good drivers represented on the right ('advanced drivers')

Your objective is to keep in the right hand side of the graph.

To achieve any goal it is essential to aim higher.

If your aim is only for average (mediocrity) then average (mediocrity) is the best you can hope for and if you're still reading this I know that mediocre is not an adjective to describe you.

It follows that your aim should be the very highest.
You may not achieve perfection because in driving terms
the perfect driver simply does not exist,
but what is the point of aiming to be average.

So, that statement above might be modified to read;

if something is worth doing it's worth doing **to the best of our ability**

'Roadcraft'

A long time ago in the 1950's the Metropolitan Police Driving School at Hendon created a manual designed for police driver training.
It was first made available to the general public in 1967.
This book has been updated many times since but remains the definitive text for developing driving skills.

'Roadcraft' forms the basis of all advanced driving instruction in this country

Now I know that you have no ambition to become a 'rapid response driver' with flashing blue lights and a two tone siren, but doesn't it make sense to cast your driving skills in the same mould as the very best?

Really good driving is a constant and lifelong 'pursuit of excellence' even though excellence may never actually be achieved.

I strongly advise you to obtain a copy of **'Roadcraft'**. Its cost equates to a couple of gallons of petrol but its value is inestimable.

You may enjoy reading it straight through but its real value is as a reference book. I regularly refer to mine. Incidentally I bought my first copy in 1977 and didn't actually take an advanced driving test until 30 years later.

In a nutshell the core principals of **Roadcraft** are
- **hazard identification**
- **hazard management using**
- **'the system of driving'**.

A hazard is anything whatsoever which has the potential to interrupt smooth steady progress of your car in a straight line.

For example, a corner, or a traffic island.

There can be stationary hazards such as a parked car or a road junction and moving hazards such as a cyclist, another moving vehicle or a pedestrian on the pavement.

'The System' is a very simple thought process which **can be applied to each and every hazard which can arise in order to maximise the efficient and safe negotiation of that hazard.**

Does that sound simple? That's because it is - brilliantly simple! However it does mean completely changing your approach to driving and change is something that we humans tend to resist beyond all logic. At first you will find it difficult to remember and difficult to put into effect, which may lead to your becoming impatient and dismissive of the whole idea. After a time you will realise just how brilliant it is and after further practice it will first of all become natural and later subconscious

There are 5 parts to the system. [chapter 2 of Roadcraft]
Later on in this book I will be devoting a whole section to each separate part so that you can fully understand the nuances of each. Does that now sound awfully complicated? I assure you it isn't but a full understanding is necessary in order to implement it fully.

In the meantime I will simply enumerate the 5 different parts and illustrate them by an example which applies each one to a simple right hand turn.

The System is   **Information**   I
                      Position   P
                      Speed   S
                      Gear   G
                      Acceleration   A

Applying this to that right hand turn;

Information (this isn't just at the beginning but continues throughout the manoeuvre)

a) received. Identify the road features, other vehicles on both sides of the road and in the side-road including their estimated speed, any pedestrians, the condition of the road surface and any adverse camber, any possible change in sun position which could cause dazzle. Check all three mirrors

Information b) given. Signal your intention to turn right.

Position. Move to the centre of the carriageway in good time without crossing the white line.

Speed. Using your brakes reduce to an appropriate speed to make the move smoothly <u>before</u> you actually start to make the turn.

Gear. Now (not before) engage the appropriate gear for that speed.

Acceleration. As you turn the steering wheel the car naturally decelerates so by very gentle throttle application the speed is maintained and then gradually increased <u>keeping the car stable</u>. This stability is maintained throughout the whole manoeuvre by using the throttle.

I can imagine you're thinking
> "What an unnecessary lot of nonsense –
> It may be O.K. for a novice but I have years of experience"
> "I already do all those things naturally"

But do you actually <u>always</u> do <u>all of those things</u> and <u>in that order</u>? Hmmmm.

> " So What?" you say.

99.9 times out of a hundred it doesn't really matter all that much. The object of The System is

> **to ensure that in the rare event of something unexpected happening you are in total control and able to respond and to deal with it in the most effective safe way.**

Stick with it. Believe me, once The System becomes second nature your driving will be much, much smoother and much, much safer engendering a justified pride in your ability and consequent increased enjoyment.

The Highway Code

There is an unfortunate misconception that the Highway Code is purely for learner drivers. I accept that definition only in the context that to excel at any skill requires one to remain a lifelong learner. The Highway Code is a mine of information which is constantly being updated to take account of changing conditions.

> **Everyone who is serious about good driving should possess an up-to-date copy and refer to it regularly to maintain good practice and knowledge**

Principles, Skills and Strategies

For the purpose of explanation, driving ability can be split into three areas, principles. skills and strategies although in practice the three are intimately related.

Principles

It is important to get your thinking straight about some factors which may be controversial or at least open to 'interpretation'.

The Law. The advanced driving test is absolutely unequivocal about this. However good a driver may otherwise be, if they break the law they will fail, period. This applies to such things as inappropriately crossing a double white line, ignoring a stop sign or red light or exceeding the speed limit; the speed limit applies to the whole of the area between the restriction and de-restriction signs.
May I suggest another reason for compliance?
Making a habit of adhering to all speed restrictions is <u>a discipline.</u>
This discipline will greatly <u>enhance your mindset</u>, your overall concentration and your development of better driving habits.
Yes I know that sometimes speed limits seem to be unnecessary but try telling that to the judge! Furthermore the amount of time you might save by a small infringement is miniscule. It's interesting that

most people quite happily accept and adhere to that 'few mph over' but rebel against the actual limit. How much time do they save? Cheshire Police did an interesting test; 2 police cars set off together to do a 25 mile journey. One obeyed all speed limits, the other drove on blue lights and siren as fast as possible.
Arrival time was just 90 seconds apart.

Other drivers. It is an unfortunate fact that getting behind the wheel of a car can in some cases cause a complete change in character. This can make otherwise calm, polite people aggressive and competitive and unfortunately such behaviour can be contagious. We live in a competitive world where self assertion is often regarded as a virtue and the route to success

Driving should never under any circumstances be competitive.

Fortunately quiet, calm politeness is also contagious.
Next time you're tempted to react negatively to another driver imagine that you might meet them socially next week.

It is a good principal to try to never do anything which might cause another driver to brake or swerve.

Distractions. I hope you're not one of those who has lucky mascots dangling from your rear view mirror, although you may have had an air freshener attached by the car wash.
If so may I offer you some scientific enlightenment?
The human brain is at all times subject to sensory bombardment from multiple sources – eyes, ears, nose, and skin to name a few. The brain cannot possibly process all of this input so it filters out the least important signals and concentrates on those of paramount importance.   A mother might sleep through a thunderstorm but wake at the smallest cry from her baby.

If an 'unimportant object' is constantly moving, even slightly, within your field of vision your brain will filter it out, rapidly creating a 'blind spot' in your brain <u>which you will not be aware of.</u>
What happens if a child steps off the pavement straight into your blind spot?

Get rid of the danglers!

Mobile phones. I hope I don't need to tell you about hand-held mobile phones but hands free phones can also be a dangerous distraction, so consider telling the caller that you will ring them back or pull off the road to complete the conversation.

Radio Soothing music may be acceptable but more strident high tempo music is best avoided. I also recommend avoiding verbal radio programmes. How would you feel if you became aware that the pilot of your holiday jet was listening to the news whilst landing your plane? For that matter neither would you want him to be discussing his plans for the weekend with his co-pilot and much less having an argument with him about an unconnected matter. Landing a jumbo jet is arguably less dangerous than driving in rush-hour traffic. I am not a very sociable person when I am driving and I try to keep the conversation to a minimum when a passenger.

Worries unconnected with the journey don't afflict us voluntarily and can't be switched off at will. However they can profoundly affect our concentration level and judgement which should be recognised and allowed for.

Tiredness and discomfort have already been mentioned but are worth mentioning again as their onset increases with age, and don't forget the full bladder. They can be very distracting and need to be minimised by sensible forward planning.

Skills

The term 'driving skill' tends to be applied to the whole 'art' of driving but in this context I am differentiating the term to apply it to the actual logistics and mechanics of handling a car as distinct from the strategies of actual driving conditions which will be discussed later. Skills could be learned on a piece of waste land or an empty car park without involving other vehicles. When we first learn to drive these skills seem extremely difficult but after a while with practice and familiarity they become firstly easy and then subconscious when they are known as **habits.**

Habits are acquired patterns of behaviour which happen automatically or subconsciously. There can be good habits and bad habits.

Good habits are commonly referred to as **skills.**

All established drivers have habits some of which are very deeply ingrained. These habits on the whole may be reasonably good but, equally so, you may have habits which, whilst not being actually bad, could nevertheless be significantly improved.

Whether it be playing sport or a musical instrument or driving or any other field of achievement in which we may be involved, the really important thing about skills is that they must be developed

until they are performed subconsciously –

what is sometimes called 'Unconscious Competence'.

Developing these automatic reflexes, i.e. acquiring a new habit, **requires time** because in order to achieve this, the brain has to establish new physical connections.   New brain connections need of the order of 2 weeks to become fully developed.   This is the medical reason why so called 'crash courses' over a short period of time are not good at creating lasting skills.   Spreading out the learning process over time is more effective.   It also explains why the conscious effort needed to change a poor habit to a good one may initially appear to cause temporary deterioration before things gets better.

I will be suggesting some changes of technique which may seem strange and at first even counterproductive.   However

These are all techniques which have been proved over many years to be the smoothest, safest and best

Equilibrium

A car is at its most stable when travelling in a straight line at a constant speed on a level surface. There are many factors which can disturb this equilibrium. Some of these are out of our control – change in camber or surface, wind etc but four of them represent

THE DRIVING SKILLS

STEERING   BRAKING   THROTTLE   GEAR CHANGING

Any of these can individually disturb the cars equilibrium but all are necessary. What is within our control however is <u>when</u> they are applied. Applying two disturbing factors simultaneously multiplies the potential danger, consequently *as far as is practical*

**the aim should be, to separate these actions
and to avoid overlapping any of them.**

Applying this principle to the above example of a right hand turn; many drivers in making this manoeuvre will brake, change gear and steer all at the same time. If something unexpected enters the equation (such as a diesel spillage or loose gravel reducing adhesion) control may be lost.

As so often happens in life, sound rules are subject to exceptions, but it is also true that "the exception proves the rule". What this enigmatic statement means is "just by being an exception implies that for the majority of the time the rule should be followed".

An example of this is the 'never overlap' principle.
It is inappropriate for me to start to explain here what the exceptions are because this section is headed 'principles' and principles is what we are concerned with.   If you want to look further into overlapping look at the section in **'Roadcraft'** pages 37 – 39.
The important thing is that, if it is used then

"overlapping must be part of a <u>planned</u> approach to a hazard".

Steering

It is probably true to say that the majority of 'average' drivers will have developed sloppy steering habits and this is an area where great improvements can be made. Why does it matter? Modern cars are extremely easy to steer and most of the time there is little danger of losing control; *most of the time*!

The trouble is that, by definition, emergency situations, arise out of the blue with no warning and if they are to be handled effectively and safely split seconds count.

A good driver is always ready to react instantly to all situations.

The best steering control is achieved with both hands gripping the wheel and positioned at 10 to 2.

Grip firmly using all the fingers and thumb.
Avoid gripping too tightly

Steering technique

This should be honed to facilitate maintaining the 10 to 2 position for the majority of the time.

The elbow should never be rested on the sill or the arm rest

Both hands should remain on the wheel at all times except for a minimum of time when changing gear with a manual transmission. Don't hold the gear stick anticipating a gear change.

Develop the 'Pull Push Technique'.

To turn left.

a) Whilst gripping with R hand slide the L hand up to 12 0'clock.
b) the L hand grips the wheel and moves to 8 0'clock **pulling** the wheel whilst grip of R hand is released
at the same time the R hand slides down to 5 o'clock
c) the R hand grips the wheel and **pushes** it to 1 o'clock whilst the grip of L hand is released and it moves back to 12 o'clock

a) to c) can be repeated as necessary.

Both hands remain on the wheel in the optimum position allowing further adjustments in either direction

['Roadcraft' pages 114 – 115]

At this moment I can imagine you thinking "Why on earth make a simple thing like steering so complicated and potentially confusing?"

What I want you to grasp is the principle of how this technique works. In practice, when you have mastered the principle you will find that the steering wheel can be smoothly fed through your two hand, both of which remain positioned where they can be used most effectively.

Far from being a series of separate steps it is a smooth flowing motion which is always under control.

Neither hand ever goes past 12 o'clock.

Apart from maintaining optimum control of the steering wheel there is another very good reason for this; If a collision were to occur the safety bags would deploy at a speed of about 200 mph.   An arm positioned past 12 o'clock would be propelled into the drivers face at this speed.   That's some punch!

In these circumstances it is not unknown for a wristwatch having to be surgically removed from a victims face.

The 'exceptions to the rule' are

- When making minor adjustments or negotiating gentle curves rather than bends - use 'rotational' steering gripping with both hands (neither going past 12 o'clock)

- When manoeuvring at very slow speed, e.g. when parking, it is permissible to cross the hands.

Once having completed a turn the next step is to return to a straight line.

This should be achieved by the same action of feeding the wheel through the two hands in the reverse direction always maintaining grip with one hand.

Never allow the wheel to centre automatically by just by releasing your grip

[N.B. Do not try to emulate the steering technique of Formula 1 drivers. The 'gearing' of the steering mechanism of racing cars is entirely different from that of road cars, necessitating a totally different technique]

Braking

There are some circumstances when speed may be controlled and sometimes reduced by use of gears and the accelerator pedal – this will be covered in detail later but

**when a decisive reduction in speed is required
this should be achieved by use of the brakes**.

There is a rather subtle distinction here and it is important to understand the difference.

As a general rule if something occurs which requires a positive slowing of the car rather than just speed reduction, then braking is appropriate.

'Brakes are for slowing, gears are for going'.

Braking occurs in three circumstances;

Approaching a hazard.   Coming to a halt.   In an emergency.

APPROACHING A HAZARD

As previously stated avoid steering and braking simultaneously

Braking should always be in a straight line

Breaking in a corner is poor driving; if it occurs it suggests that you are driving too fast or in too high a gear

COMING TO A HALT Application of the brakes will always cause the nose of the car to dip.

Similarly when the car comes to a halt the reverse motion happens. These rock and roll movements should be kept to a minimum; they are uncomfortable and also potentially destabilising.
To achieve this requires careful controlled use of the brake pedal.

initiate braking gently.
Progressively increase pedal pressure, until almost stopped.
On approaching the halt release the pedal gently.

The hand brake should always be applied when the car is stationary for more than a few moments, for example at a red traffic light.

This applies to both manual and automatic boxes

It should not be used for brief pauses such as the approach to a junction, unless you are on a hill.

Using a manual gearbox,

**when the brake has been applied select neutral.
To start off again engage 1st gear
then release the handbrake as you move off**

In an automatic

**the handbrake should be applied but the gear left in drive.
To start merely release the handbrake.**

IN AN EMERGENCY   Brake as hard as you can.

This will activate the ABS (anti-lock braking system)
This doesn't help the braking but is designed to prevent skidding;
(in an emergency situation you may well be turning).

**If you are unfamiliar with the use of ABS
it would be a good idea to try it out in a safe situation**

Gears and Throttle

In my early days of motoring and I expect yours too, cars were very different from today's models and to achieve the best performance required a much higher level of positive driver input.
Modern cars by comparison are much easier to drive and this can sometimes produce a lackadaisical approach.
This particularly applies to the use of gears.
 Modern engines will pull over a wide range of revolutions and this can result in lazy gear changing and considerable loss of efficiency.

An engine operates most efficiently in the middle range commonly called the **'power band'**. When running within this range it can both accelerate and decelerate comfortably.
Fuel consumption at steady speed is also at the most economical in this range.   Many people believe that by using high gears as often as possible better fuel consumption will result and this idea is reinforced in some cars by 'economical gear indictors'.
This is not necessarily so.

For fuel economy the most important factors are

**not driving too fast and
avoiding hard acceleration particularly when starting off.**

It should also always be remembered that modern cars
when decelerating in gear do not use any fuel at all.

Conversely an engine which has to work hard at low revs because the gear is too high burns more fuel.

In order to be able to respond rapidly to any circumstance requiring variation of speed

The ideal is to always remain within the power band

Modern cars are almost always equipped with a rev counter which can help in acquiring this sympathy with the car. The power band varies from car to car but is usually around 2,000 to 3,500 revs However knowing where the power band is, is predominantly a matter of 'feel' - an awareness that the car feels relaxed and comfortable, ready to accelerate or decelerate at the command of the throttle.

In a 30 mph zone most cars operate most efficiently in 3rd gear

Manual changes
In the old days in order to execute a smooth gear change it was essential to synchronize the engine revs and the gearbox revs using the process of 'double de-clutching'. Nowadays with synchro-mesh this is no longer necessary, however it is good practice and conducive to smooth progress, when changing gear to cultivate a sensitivity to engine speed. This is much less stressful to both engine and gearbox and consequently also to the occupants of the car.
 When changing down, very briefly pause in neutral whilst maintaining throttle pressure to increase engine revs to the level anticipated by the lower gear before engaging the gear.
This is known as a 'sustained gear change'.
Similarly, when changing up, allow the engine revs to drop and engage the gear at the point of synchronization.

Block Changes It is not necessary to 'go through the gears' when making a marked change in road speed. Judge the correct speed to negotiate the hazard then select the appropriate gear.

Automatics. Many drivers of cars with automatic gearboxes simply put the gear stick in 'Drive' and never do anything else until they park. These gear boxes are marvellously designed and are perfectly capable of performing pretty well under these circumstances but do these drivers ever wonder why the gear lever offers some other options?

**Using an automatic gearbox intelligently will
improve performance,
increase safety and
enhance the driving experience**

There are many variations in type and performance of automatic gearboxes. It is important to read the vehicle handbook to familiarise yourself with the characteristics of your car.

In the normal 'Drive' mode an automatic gear box will always tend to up-shift whenever the load is off the drive, for example when a bend in the road causes the driver to lift his foot from the throttle.
The consequences are

    a) a gear change may occur whilst the vehicle is turning

    b) just when extra power is needed to draw the car round the bend the engaged gear is too high [see later section on 'acceleration sense']

The answer is to either engage the 'Sport' mode or to manually change down and hold a lower gear throughout the hazard.

The same applies on a downhill stretch. In order to take advantage of engine braking and avoid overheating the brakes it is essential to hold a lower gear.

When descending hills select a gear which allows a minimum of braking.
This applies to both automatic and manual boxes

Unconscious Competence

To hone and improve your driving performance, the four basic skills
   steering, braking, gear changing and acceleration
require to be assessed and perhaps new refined techniques mastered. This takes time and effort and it is probably wise to concentrate on one at a time until they become your new habits.

Any change of habit at first seems less than comfortable and the benefits are only really felt and appreciated when the habit is fully established.

Patience and resolve are the watchwords

A bad habit which you have been unaware of can be described as
   'Unconscious Incompetence'. Once you're aware of it,
it becomes   **'Conscious Incompetence'**.   By trying to correct it,
it becomes   **'Conscious competence'**   and when it's become a new habit it is **'Unconscious competence'**

Your aim should be for all your driving skills to become
Unconsciously competent

All that is required is an attitude of mind and practice

Strategies

Improving habits and creating skills is the starting point of good driving but I stress that this is 'the starting point'.
Skills are absolutely essential but

Good skills are only the basis upon which really good performance can be developed;

The other essential requirement is the development of good strategies. Strategies are concerned with interaction with road conditions and other road users and are primarily concerned with

SAFETY.

**Safety is the be-all and end-all of advanced driving –
It is the overriding measure of competence and
equates with good strategies**

Whereas skills should be developed to the level of unconscious competence, **strategies are all about concentration;**
The more that we concentrate the better we will become.
Another way of looking at it is; skills are the physical aspect of driving whilst strategies are the mental aspects.

Strategies are the planning and execution of manoeuvres to deal with all situations and events that arise.

Or in other words

**Hazard identification and
Hazard management**

Hazards are infinitely variable and this is where **The System** comes into play. Information; Position; Speed; Gear; Acceleration.   IPSGA. This can be applied to every possible scenario.

'I' Information

A radio will only broadcast programmes if it is switched on. Similarly, although drivers may 'react' to a red light, if they are not concentrating they may completely miss a mass of other information.

**In all motoring collisions lack of
concentration is probably the
single most important contributory factor.**

The most common word occurring in insurance claims is *"suddenly"*. Only about 5% of so called accidents are wholly accidental in that

**if somebody involved had done something different
the collision could have been avoided and
the consequences prevented**.

The highway authorities and the police nowadays call them RTCs – **R**oad **T**raffic **C**ollisions rather than accidents.

Out there in the world many drivers frequently, mentally 'switch off' because their thoughts are elsewhere and in effect they start to drive using only their subconscious skills.

They switch to 'auto-pilot'.

They are in fact driving with a lack of attention because their attention is elsewhere.

Driving 'without due care and attention' is a criminal offence but it only gets penalised when a collision results.

It is arguably equally culpable when nothing untoward ensues.

N.B It should also be recognised that if the mind is occupied with the development and performance of skills, then this will to a degree detract from giving 100% attention to other matters.
This underlines the importance of developing automatic skills.

Advanced drivers develop and maintain a high level of concentration

They constantly '**read the road**' ahead gathering information which enables them to anticipate events in advance of them happening.
This is known as OBSERVATION
Observation uses all the senses,
looking <u>and seeing</u>,
listening <u>and hearing</u>.

<u>Visual observation</u> should be

Focused but not fixated (e.g. on the vehicle in front)

Scanning everything visible. This includes close, medium and far distance, to the sides and the rear view mirrors.

Limit Points

One of the most difficult things when driving on unfamiliar country roads is to judge the severity of bends, often obscured by foliage. The next time you are out on a country road, as you approach a bend, mentally take note of how much you can see along each side of the road .

The farthest point you can see on the outside of the bend and the farthest point you can see on the inside of the bend will coincide and this is known as the' limit point'.

Keep watching this point and as you approach the bend you will see that at first it is stationary but as you get nearer it starts to 'run away from you' as the bend opens up. The speed that it moves is dependant of the sharpness of the bend; on a tight bend it moves slowly, on a gentle bend it moves quickly.

Bearing in mind the adage "always be able to stop within the distance you can see, the secret is to adjust your speed to the speed that the limit point is moving.   This may sound difficult but in practice is very easy and helpful .

Try it.

Auditory observation includes traffic sounds, horns and sirens your engine noise and information from your passenger and sat nav.

Forward Planning

Good observation predicts happenings with a long 'time horizon'.
(the time between the observation and the happening)

The' time horizon' may be 10 seconds or so and is continuously updating.
If the time horizon is getting too short then reduce speed.

Thinking must always be ahead of the present situation.
It predicts what others are likely to do but should always leave room for people to change their mind.

Never put your car where your eyes and brain haven't been before.

OBSERVATION LINKS.   It is an interesting exercise to interpret apparently small clues to indicate future happenings and it is very rewarding when that event actually transpires.   We call these clues observation links A list of some of them can be found in the appendix.

You should learn to be constantly planning your route ahead, particularly through complicated junctions.

At junctions the approach road-sign will indicate the number of the road on which you intend to exit. This number is often painted on the road surface in the correct lanes indicating an easily followed route through the junction.

The result of proper forward planning is

PROACTIVE, SMOOTH, CALM PROGRESS

in contrast to a succession of rushed reactions

Everyone is familiar with the sportsman who seems always to have more time than the opposition. That's all about anticipation.

Conversely how often do we hear people complaining that
"driving is stressful".
I suspect that the stress is induced by constantly being taken by surprise by events and the actions of others.

INFORMATION SHOULD BE GIVEN AS WELL AS RECEIVED

Telegraph your intentions clearly

- E.g. Use brake lights before slowing for a speed limit or passing a cyclist,
- Indicate in good time but not too early.
- Eye contact is particularly valuable.
- Avoid hesitation and indecision.
- If in doubt that someone has seen you,
  e.g. a child near the curb - peep your horn.
- Use headlights in the day time if the visibility is poor,
  e.g. if it's raining hard enough to need continuous wipers.
- Be aware of other people's blind spots not forgetting left-hand drivers

HEADLIGHT FLASHES
The Highway Code states

"Only flash your headlights to let other road users know that you are there. Do not flash your headlights to convey any other message or to intimidate other road users"
"Never assume that flashing headlights is a signal inviting you to proceed. Use your own judgement and proceed carefully"

Although headlight flashes can seem courteous and helpful they can easily be misinterpreted so think twice before using them.
If a collision ensued you could be held responsible.

P' Position

Always position you vehicle in such a way as to.

    a) **Cause minimal inconvenience to other vehicles.**
    b) **Facilitate your own speed and change of direction**
    c) **Maximise space**

STATIONARY TRAFFIC AHEAD

'Tyres and Tarmac'. When halting you should stop in such a position that allows you to see the tyres of the car in front plus a bit of road. In the event of the car in front stalling you will have room to pull round it.

IN MOVING TRAFFIC

Following distance. One of the commonest faults seen on the road is driving too close to the vehicle in front- commonly called 'tail-gating.' This is not only dangerous but causes aggravation to the driver in front.

**If you are a victim of tailgating I suggest you
let the idiot get past out of your way.**

The safe separation distance varies with speed and should be measured in seconds.

**The minimum separation to allow for
reaction time and braking time is 2 seconds**

In poor conditions (poor visibility, a slippery road surface, corners, tiredness) **much more should be allowed.**

To judge a 2 second gap Choose a marker ahead, either on the road or the verge, (e.g. a paint-mark, a post or a shadow). Count the time interval between the car in front passing the mark and yourself.

2 seconds can be judged by saying to yourself;

"Zero, One thousand, 2 thousand" or
"Only a fool breaks the 2 second rule"

Position when Negotiating hazards

Every hazard is different. Positioning requires the driver to bear in mind the principles in bold type at the beginning of this section. It must always be remembered that the different parts of IPSGA all inter-react with each other.

When negotiating bends on rural roads in the absence of other traffic, take the 'racing line' which smoothes out the bend by approaching at the outside of the bend, moves to the apex, then back to the outer side.

As a method of to explaining 'P' I propose
as an example to go into considerable detail on

THE ART OF NEGOTIATING ROUNDABOUTS

[it might be helpful to read The Highway Code sections 184 – 190]

The principles of roundabout negotiation are primarily concerned with correct positioning. Once properly understood these principles can be applied to most other hazards.

Motor Insurance Company Statistics indicate that 'incidents' occur most commonly on roundabouts.

Why should this be so?

First   CONFUSION arising from the wide diversity of roundabouts, which include mini roundabouts, multiple roundabouts and a huge variation in size and number of junctions.

Second   IGNORANCE of correct techniques.

Third   POOR CONCENTRATION

In order to avoid becoming part of the aforementioned statistics, we all need to thoroughly <u>understand the principles involved, and how they can be applied in all circumstances</u> .

It will also help us to be aware of and avoid other vehicles behaving unpredictably on roundabouts .

Firstly a word about 'I' - Information on traffic islands.

<u>**Information a) Received**</u>

It is essential **to be fully aware of all vehicles nearby.**
Look out for their <u>signals</u> and their <u>position,</u>
(always allowing for them to be wrong).
Use all mirrors, particularly the left door-mirror before exiting the roundabout

<u>**Information b) Given.**</u> Your position is most important in indicating your intentions to others.
Signals must be correct.
<u>Wrong signals are worse than no signal</u>!

<u>Information</u> starts at the approach sign
- **Plan you route through the roundabout.**
  Identify your exit. Note the road number and nearest destination, E.g. "3rd exit, A 51 Nantwich" (being aware that road numbers may be in 2 directions)
- **Identify the correct entry lane.** (See below)
- **Consider if a signal is appropriate.**

*Information is constantly updated throughout the manoeuvre,
as a consequence of which ;*

Position is constantly being reviewed and changed.

- **Select the correct lane.**
- **DO NOT change lanes without extreme care and only if it will not affect other vehicles.**

[If you find yourself in the wrong lane in closely moving traffic you may have to continue round the roundabout past your intended exit, or conversely you may have to exit early before turning round and retracing your steps]

> **NEVER 'UNDERTAKE'** unless the lane on your right is paused or moving very slowly

The most important thing, particularly on busy roundabouts is being in the right lane

In order to understand the basics lets imagine a simple cross- roads with an island;

access   - 6 o'clock

exits   - 9 o'clock, 12 o'clock and 3 o'clock

(Often there may be 2, 4 or even 5 exits, not set at right angles but the same principles will apply.)

We are going to consider positioning in four circumstances

APPROACHING
ENTERING
CIRCULATING
EXITING

1.Positioning WHEN APPROACHING

A. To exit at 9 o'clock. (The first exit)

Position on approach. <u>Always</u> the lane nearest to the Left.

Information on approach Received – give way to traffic from the R
Given   - signal left.

B. To exit at 3 o'clock

Position on approach. <u>Always</u> the lane nearest the Right.

Information on approach Received – give way to traffic from R
Given   - signal right

C. To exit anywhere between A and B

Position on approach. **3 lane approaches** will always be defined by white lines and usually have lane identification painted on the road by arrows or road numbers.

2 lane approaches.

Sometimes the left lane has a left arrow in which case take the R lane.

Otherwise (in the absence of lane markings);

Base your decision on the approach sign -
>   If your exit is 'after 12 o'clock' - Take the right hand lane.
>   Up to and including 12 o'clock - Take the left hand lane
>   Except on busy 2 lane approaches, with slow traffic in the left lane when it is permitted to use the right lane.

Information on approach received – give way to traffic from the R
>   given - **DO NOT SIGNAL at this point**!

---

2. Positioning WHEN ENTERING

Information.   " Ready to stop - Looking to go"

Speed   IF ENTRY IS CLEAR, MAINTAIN MOMENTUM.
>   Do not stop unless there's a halt sign (unusual).

Gear   Select appropriate gear.   Usually 2nd, occasionally 3rd.
>   Automatics engage 'sport mode'

---

3. Positioning WHEN CIRCULATING

Accelerator   Maintain gentle positive throttle to balance the car.

Position Where lane markings exist (Applies to all 'big' roundabouts).
>   Following them will lead seamlessly to your exit.
>   Be aware that other vehicles may hide the on-road markings.

>   In the absence of lane markings treat each section of the roundabout as a 2 lane section of a dual carriageway,

i.e. **only change lanes with due consideration of other vehicles.** However, in the absence of other traffic and if there is no risk of conflict or confusion with other road users, it is good practice to 'straight line' or 'trim the corners' in order to enhance stability and progress.

"Nothing about – straighten it out".

Position   Immediately after passing the junction before your intended exit;

signal left and then move to the left hand lane, always assuming that this lane is clear.

On some busy dual carriageways this will not be possible and both lanes will feed into the two lanes of the exit road.

In this case signal L as above.

---

4. Positioning WHEN EXITING

Information   Always check your left wing mirror before turning left. (You should already be signalling)

Position   *If in the left hand lane*
exit into the left hand lane of the exit road.
If on a busy road with two lanes feeding into the exit road and you are in the right hand lane,
you must keep to the right hand lane of the exit road.

Failure to comply with this is one of the reasons for all those 'comings together' mentioned in the first paragraph.

[Be aware that in this respect the diagram in the Highway Code, para 185 is unfortunately confusing.   It suggests that you can use either lane of the exit road.   However the diagram only applies to a very small island where the possibility of two vehicles wishing to use the same exit does not exist]

NOTE   Frequently when two exit lanes exist they merge into one lane very quickly.   In this case drivers should adopt the 'zip' principle, taking alternate turns.

All this may sound confusing but the essence lies in the first step

> **'Plan you route through the roundabout'.**

Now back to considering the different parts of IPSGA

'S&G '- Speed & Gear

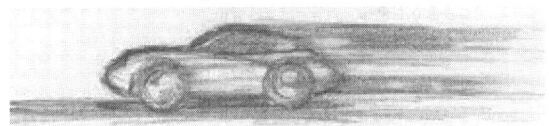

In this respect we are considering speed primarily in the context of its role in **The System ('IPSGA')** , that is the method of executing a manoeuvre to negotiate a hazard.

It is part of *foreword planning* and requires the driver to

> **use judgement in determining the appropriate speed
> to negotiate the hazard in safety.**

This is a matter of experience and little more needs to be said apart from stressing the sequence of events.

> **First adjust position,**
> **then adjust speed**
> **then select the appropriate gear.**

What is the appropriate gear?
We have already discussed the power band on page 22

> **Select the appropriate gear to remain in the power band.**

The manoeuvre can now be completed in the most efficient manner.

It should be appreciated that conditions are continually changing and that as a result of information received (**'I'**),one hazard often tends to merge into the next so that speed (**'S'**) may need to be modified. This should have has been anticipated in the initial gear selection (**'G'**) which should be able to avoid more than one change.

> **Speed adjustments can be made purely using the throttle.('A')**

This will be discussed more fully in the section later on 'Acceleration Sense'

Whilst on the topic of speed through hazards I want to take the opportunity of expanding the discussion to discuss the whole, somewhat thorny and slightly controversial topic of speed.
Speed is a topic where there often seems to be s a strange dichotomy in that whereas most people agree that others drive too fast and that speed is a frequent cause of 'accidents' at the same time we do not always apply the same criteria to ourselves.

Let's be very blunt about this, we are talking about **RISK.**

Risk of collision and risk of the consequences which can include
life changing injuries and death.
To repeat the statistics
Every day in this country on average 5 people are killed in motoring incidents and another 60 have life changing injuries.

The trouble is that many of us tend to think that 'accidents' happen to other people and not to ourselves. Let's have a look at what the chance of a collision, the risk, actually entails.

$$\text{Chance of collision} = \frac{\text{Speed} \times \text{Surprise}}{\text{Separation}}$$

Controlling risk = Keeping the equation in balance

Good driving is **Active Risk Management**

If you take away nothing else from this book please remember
This simple equation and keep it constantly in mind.

**In the majority of motoring incidents excessive speed
and driving too close are significant if not primary factors.**

More on Speed

1. *Excessive speed.*

Is *e*xceeding the speed limit and is always Illegal

It may not actually be dangerous!

2. *Inappropriate speed.*

Driving within the speed limit but too fast for the conditions

Not illegal but always dangerous!

The golden rule is to
adjust your speed to any and all circumstances.

Speed limits represent reasonable target speeds in ideal conditions

In adverse conditions, darkness, rain, fog, frost etc
speed should be reduced accordingly

It is almost as important to keep up to speed particularly in heavy traffic.

If a whole stream of traffic is travelling above the
speed limit there is no safer option than compliance

The Highway Code advises that we should always be able to stop "within the distance we can see".

That's all well and good but **may not allow for the other driver coming the other way** at the same speed.

The distance travelled during the time it
takes to react depends on the speed.

[Speed in mph x 1 ½ = distance in feet per second]

SURPRISE
Anything which is unpredicted is a potential risk

In the equation above

>speed and surprise don't just add together;
>when either increases the other is multiplied.

Surprise is anything that happens which hasn't been anticipated.

>**Surprise is the greatest source of danger**
>Always expect the unexpected.

The corner stone of good driving is ANTICIPATION.

>[Far more important than "having fast reflexes"]

SEPARATION (SPACE)

Collisions happen when **someone runs out of space**.

>Arbitrary measurements can be dangerous.
>Every situation must be judged on its merits.

The Golden rules are –

>allow sufficient space for the circumstances
>AND for the anticipated circumstances.

Be aware of 'diminishing' spaces and compensate for them.

Remember the 2 second minimum following distance.

OVERTAKING SPACE

Higher speeds require more space.

The overtaken object must be allowed for –
Give more space to cyclists, learner drivers, and ditherers.

Your immediate 'forward plan' should cover at least 10 seconds
Never compete for space

OVERTAKING SPEED

Speed limits don't make an exception when overtaking.
This must be taken into consideration when planning an overtake.
For example it would be extremely difficult to overtake a vehicle travelling at 55 without exceeding 60.

A difference of at least 10 mph between the speed limit and the speed of the slower vehicle is necessary.

This is the absolute minimum in good conditions on a straight road. Often the differential needs to be much higher.
Following a slow vehicle can be frustrating, however it should be realised that that it represents a 'moving hazard' and that

Overtaking is a high-risk, complicated manoeuvre

Because of this, in this instance, I suggest that the whole section on overtaking in **Roadcraft** (pages 185 -210) should be carefully studied.

This will reinforce your appreciation of just how complicated overtaking is and encourage you to always ask yourself

a) Do I really need to overtake?
b) is an overtake a reasonable possibility?

Very often the intelligent answer to these 2 questions will be "No". If this is so, a calm acceptance of the situation will allow you to proceed contentedly at a slightly reduced rate of progress.

Acceleration Sense
The 'A' of the System

Acceleration sense is A COMBINATION OF SKILL AND STRATEGY and is one of the most important features of advanced driving. It should be fully understood and practiced until it becomes second nature. Acceleration sense can apply to nearly all driving situations and is the safest, most economical, most ecological and most satisfying of driving techniques.

Acceleration sense is the ability to vary the vehicle speed in response to changing road or traffic conditions by accurate use of the accelerator, using the brakes little or not at all.

Although acceleration comes at the end of IPSGA it is not just the final stage of **The System** but is an integral part of good driving and a proper understanding and practice of this skill is fundamental to expert car control.

Being in the right gear is an essential prerequisite.

To grasp the concept of acceleration sense fully it is helpful to have some knowledge of physics, in particular of the forces which influence any lump of matter whilst it is in motion and the effect that these forces have on the way it behaves.

**A car is at its most stable when travelling in
a straight line with the engine just pulling**

A car travelling in a straight line has **momentum**, which is a product of its weight and its speed.

Momentum wants to continue travelling in a straight line (↑).
[*The greater the momentum (speed x weight) the more difficult it is to change its direction.*]

Other forces affecting the car's straight line course are

- **engine drive** (↑).
- **wheel friction** with the road surface (↓) - this is influenced by the quality of the tyres and the 'slipperiness' of the road surface .
- **air resistance** (↓)
- **wind resistance** (which depends on wind direction)

to maintain a steady straight line speed the driver

subconsciously **balances all these forces with the throttle.**

In a straight line all the forces (apart from wind effect) act in line with the tyre tread.

WHAT HAPPENS WHEN THE STEERING WHEEL IS TURNED?
In a left-hand turn
the friction effect (↓) is diverted across the tread (✓).
It also increases in size.
This increase slows the car's speed slightly and acts with the momentum to create deviation.

Momentum ↑ + Friction ✓ = Deviation ↖

At the same time **centrifugal force** comes into effect. Everyone is familiar with the concept of a motorcycle leaning over in a corner to  counteract this force. The same force acts on a car but a car cannot compensate like a motorcycle. The heavy upper part of the car wants to continue in a straight line, whilst the tyres (at the bottom) are in effect trying to trip the car up; the result is that the car tends to lean towards the outer side of the curve and its weight is transferred from the inner-side wheels to the outer-side wheels resulting in **loss of adhesion** and potential **under-steer** and **skidding.** This uncomfortable 'yawing' effect will be increased at higher speeds and with tightening of the curve and will be accentuated by further steering adjustment as will happen in the majority of situations.
It will be greatly increased if the brakes are applied.

Hence the importance of the 'P' and 'S' parts of IPSGA.
All excess speed should be taken off <u>before</u> entering the bend.

Fortunately there is a very simple way of correcting the problem. This is achieved by applying more turning force ↖ by using engine drive (which always acts in the same direction as the tyre tread) by the simple expedient of **applying gentle positive throttle.** The car is now **drawn into the curve**, centrifugal force is counteracted and the car remains stable with weight distributed equally through all four road wheels.

If the engine is <u>operating within the power band</u>,
giving maximum flexibility,
the car can be balanced in a level position through
a series of bends simply by use of the throttle.

TO SUMMARIZE
The majority of hazards require a change in direction.
Any curve will act to reduce speed. The aim of acceleration sense is to apply sufficient positive throttle to just counteract this reduction <u>plus a little bit more</u>. When done correctly this gives a feeling 'as if the car is negotiating the corner on rails'.

When driving an automatic gearbox, this technique can be used much more effectively when the gearbox is locked into the appropriate gear or is in 'sports mode'

A personal anecdote

Many years ago when I was a young motorcyclist I borrowed a motorcycle combination. The sidecar was mounted on the left and before I set off the owner explained to me that this prevented the normal technique of leaning a bike over to the inside of a left hand bend to counteract centrifugal force.
He explained that instead one has to "accelerate the bike round the sidecar".

A short while later I was travelling down an incline towards a left hand bend and facing a large lorry travelling in the other direction.
   The following few seconds is etched on my brain like a video.
I tried to turn and absolutely nothing happened – I just kept going straight towards the lorry.
 In the face of imminent disaster it took some courage to open the throttle hard but my friend's advice overcame my fear and the increased engine power floated me easily round the corner.

The only way a left mounted combination can negotiate a left-hand bend at even moderate pace is to apply 'position, speed, gear, **acceleration'.**
Failure to do this or application of the brakes in the corner will result in the side-car's wheel leaving the ground and the unit travelling straight on.   At worst it will flip over.

   Once learned the technique is never forgotten.
   The principal is exactly the same for a car.

Driving Environments

There is an infinite variety in both road conditions and traffic conditions and consequently

an ever present need to be alert to the necessity of modifying our driving techniques accordingly.

It is helpful to consider three different driving environments, RURAL, URBAN and MOTORWAY which have distinct differences from one another and also to realise that each of them is affected by traffic volume from very light to heavily congested.

RURAL.

The vast majority of the countries roads can be described as rural, from farm tracks to country lanes, to 'A' roads to dual carriageways. There are many more miles of rural roads than there are urban or motorway roads so that mile for mile they are comparatively less congested. Consequently it might be reasonable to assume that they should be safer. Unfortunately the facts of the matter are that rural roads account for over 60% of all road casualties.
I find this statistic worrying.
All sorts of explanations are put forward such as limited visual horizon due to bends and vegetation, slow moving vehicles like

tractors and bicycles, poor road surfaces, 60 mph being too high for some unlimited roads and so on.

**Undoubtedly a major cause is
the overtaking manoeuvre on a 2-way road**

To my mind all of these things may be contributory factors but they are not the fundamental reason.

Once again the prime factor is human error.

So rather than occupying our minds looking at causes let's accept that adverse conditions exist and concentrate our efforts on solutions.

If rural roads are statistically more dangerous that means the risk or the 'chance of collision' is higher.   Remember page 41

$$\text{Chance of collision} = \frac{\text{Speed} \times \text{Surprise}}{\text{Separation}}$$

**The solution to rural road casualties lies in
speed, concentration and anticipation.**

Anticipation unfortunately has to include making allowance for the irresponsible actions of others.

URBAN

Even if you don't actually live in a 'built up area' you won't have to drive far before one is reached and conditions change. However the second important driving environment to which I am referring is the LARGE CONURBATION where traffic is much heavier.

Here the need for proper strategies becomes the dominant factor and those skills need to be automatic.

In a strange town another factor arises; that of finding ones way. This is an area where satnav is particularly useful both for locating your destination and finding your way out of a city centre. Alternatively the route needs to be thoroughly pre-planned. A useful aid is to write road numbers across the top of your windscreen with a felt tipped pen.

Because the majority of us live in large conurbations driving in these conditions becomes the norm. (Could lack of familiarity be another reason for those increased rural road casualties?)
If you are making changes to your driving skills as a result of my previous advice it might be a good idea to spend some time on rural roads until you become unconsciously competent.

In my opinion, wherever possible, practicing and perfecting the art of driving – the skills and strategies – is most profitably undertaken on rural roads.

MOTORWAYS

In the 21St Century motorway driving in the United Kingdom is becoming progressively more stressful and frustrating.
Sadly heavy traffic density and delays are becoming the norm and whereas formerly motorways represented the optimum route for longer journeys this is no longer necessarily the case. Allowance for hold-ups must be planned for and sometimes motorways may be actively avoided. Similarly in adverse weather conditions such as fog or heavy rain at night, the wise course may be to choose an alternative route which is less stressful.
However let us assume that motorways are being used and look at the ways in which motorway driving is different.

Joining a motorway
Motorway access roads usually have two carriageways.
 This can be confusing!
If the two carriageways have clearly defined, staged access to the motorway, then either carriageway may be taken.
 If not then it is safer to approach in single file in the outer lane

Anticipate vehicles in the motorway's nearside lane to be travelling at around 60 mph (the speed of HGVs) with reasonable gaps between vehicles. In order to 'slot in' to this column of traffic

Adjust your joining speed to theirs (50 – 60 mph)

As soon as a vehicle has passed going fractionally faster than you, **accelerate to equal his speed and pull out behind him**

Remain in this lane until you and other drivers around have adjusted to the new situation.

Do not move into the middle lane immediately!

On the motorway

**Motorway traffic is high speed and dangerous.
At 70 mph you travel over 30 meters (35 yards) every second.**

Some people describe motorway driving as boring. I find this difficult to understand. To drive well and safely requires a very high level of concentration and forward planning;

**Observation should be constantly assessing conditions
as far ahead as can be seen
*and as far behind as can be seen***

This allows no time for boredom which is an indication of lack of concentration.

Information Make sure you are familiar with all the motorway signs as detailed in the **Highway Code**

Lane discipline

In freely moving motorway conditions
**whenever possible the aim should be to
drive in the left hand lane.**

This lane is frequently occupied by HGVs who are theoretically restricted to 60 mph; hence to overtake them requires moving to the middle lane. By observing a long way ahead it is possible to plan one's route to take the best advantage of the positioning of the inside lane traffic so as to **avoid frequent lane changes,** however the aim should always be to return to the inside lane when a long gap forms.

It is important to be aware of what is happening behind.

**If the road behind is empty there is
no need to return to the nearside lane**

Beware of fast moving traffic coming up to you suddenly

Lane Changes should only be made for a specific reason and should be definite and precise.
- Check the rear view mirrors
- **Signal your intention at least three seconds before the move.**
- Do a quick 'shoulder check' to make sure your blind spot is empty.
- If all is clear, move.

When the lane change is necessary in order to overtake another vehicle, as soon as you have passed and checked your left wing mirror, you can return to the same lane without signalling.

**However if the return is delayed for any reason a
left shoulder check and signal should be made.**

It is particularly important to anticipate the movements of HGV's and other vehicles in their near vicinity because when they overtake they will stay in the middle lane <u>at less than your speed</u> for some distance. This means that you will have to use the outside lane or lanes.

The movements of inside lane vehicles can be predicted by <u>constantly observing them at the limit of your vision</u>

For example, because of differences in power and load, HGV's most often overtake each other on inclines.

Also an HGV planning an overtake will move into the 'contact position' reducing the gap to the leading vehicle

<u>Junctions</u>

**Be aware of vehicles joining the motorway via the access slip road.
In order to allow them unimpeded access try to move to the middle lane in good time.**

If this move is impossible make sure that the separation distance between you and the vehicle in front of you is big enough to allow them space to join the lane.

<u>In congested, slow moving traffic</u> -

KEEP IN LANE. Trying to gain an advantage by frequent lane changes should be avoided

In these conditions many drivers drive far too close, which is the reason for 'shunts' when an RTC does occur.

If the car behind is too close to you, you will need to leave a larger gap in front in order to compensate.

It is often useful to keep slightly to the side of the vehicle in front so as to gain a view of the brake lights of the vehicles in front of him.

Blind spots
Be aware of other vehicles' blind spots and avoid sitting in them. Either pull past or drop back.
Give extra consideration to left hand drive vehicles as indicated by their advertising and number plates

Always be aware of and make allowance for the possibility of other drivers acting unpredictably

Transgressions
Examples of bad driving happen on all types of road but seem to be more prevalent on motorways where they are potentially more dangerous because of the high speeds involved.
The reasons may be ignorance, the weight of traffic, frustrations caused by delays or a perceived anonymity, but whatever the cause,

the consequence is an aggressive attitude in many drivers.

Mistakes happen to all of us, ignorance can be forgiven but aggression is never acceptable. Unfortunately it is contagious ultimately climaxing in 'road rage'. The essential thing to realise is that road rage always starts in a small way and **always involves two people** – one who initiates and another who reacts.
Road rage is fortunately fairly rare but aggression is not.

Recognised that

**Road rage starts off with mild aggression and intolerance
Nip it in the bud
Anger and aggression has no part in safe driving.**

It is inevitable that you will encounter people who drive too fast, people who tail-gate, who pull out without signalling, who overtake on a closing lane and then cut in, even people who show active aggression to you.

However eloquent your response is to this sort of behaviour may be, they can't hear you and are totally oblivious to it.

The only person to be affected is you

Get out of their way and proceed with equanimity in safety!

*Forgive us our driving mistakes as we forgive
the driving mistakes of others*

Leaving the motorway

At the one mile sign. Commence forward planning
Assess the traffic in the nearside lane. If there is a long column of HGVs you will need to choose a suitable gap to pull into but at this distance there is ample time and there is no point in slowing down to nearside lane speed too early.

Remember other vehicles may also be planning an exit.

By the half mile sign or very soon afterwards move into the nearside lane.

At the 300^x sign commence signalling left.

Do not start to reduce speed until you are on the slip road.

If your ongoing route is to the right, immediately signal right and take the right hand lane.

Otherwise take the left lane or follow road markings.

Adjust mentally to different road speeds.

Adverse Conditions

Arguably one of the most dangerous factors in motoring is

changing weather conditions and failure to adjust to them.

In very bad weather a serious consideration should be to ask oneself the question

Is my journey really necessary?

If it is, then adjustments must be made, not least in allowing much more time for the journey

As previously stated, speed limits tend to be regarded as safe limits. This is true only for ideal conditions.

Whenever conditions are less than perfect consideration should be given to further speed reduction

This consideration should always be exercised when night driving when reduced vision and dazzle from oncoming headlights will always fortify every hazard.

As well as reducing speed, separation must be increased to 5 seconds or even more

Heavy rain

Firstly, rain drastically reduces vision, particularly at night.
A particular hazard on motorways is spray thrown up by some HGVs creating an almost impenetrable visual barrier to their offside.

**In these circumstances it is imperative
to hold back until a clear view ahead is obtained,
and an overtake in the 3rd lane is possible**

Another problem is that when it is raining, because humidity is very high there in an increase tendency for all the windows to mist up thereby further diminishing visibility. This problem can take time to rectify even with effective air conditioning but should not be ignored.

Secondly, rain always reduces surface adhesion thereby increasing the stopping distance. This effect is more pronounced after a spell of dry summer weather when rubber has been laid down on the tarmac.

Motorways are prone to developing patches of standing water which at motorway speeds can cause AQUAPLANING.
Aquaplaning results in a sudden and <u>complete </u>loss of steering control; Neither braking nor steering will have the slightest effect.

**If standing water is suspected speed must be
reduced <u>drastically</u> before it is reached.**

Do not assume that because other cars are travelling
faster, that it is safe to do so.

Snow and Ice.

The above remarks about slippery roads apply to snow and ice but multiplied several times with the additional problem of patchy unpredictable conditions including 'black ice' (invisible patches of ice) Here, in addition to danger of skidding, we have the further problem of wheel-spin. To counteract this, the aim should be to

**drive in as high a gear as practical and
only accelerate very ,very gently.**

If your motoring habits involve a high proportion of winter driving you should consider investing in winter tyres, and carrying snow chains, a shovel, and some salt.
If you get stuck it may help to reduce tyre pressures and when trying to start, engage 2nd or even 3rd gear and accelerate as gently as possible. If the wheels start to spin, you must stop and try again.

High winds

On emerging from a protected area to an open road, a side wind can suddenly cause a fast moving vehicle to swerve off course. Good anticipation should be able to prevent this.
Not so expected may be when overtaking a high sided vehicle on ones 'windward' side. The sudden loss of shelter may cause your car to veer towards the overtaken vehicle.

Wet leaves

A patch of wet leaves can seriously reduce traction and as leaves tend to accumulate on sharp bends they ought to be anticipated in autumn

Sunshine

Particularly In the winter months a low sun can be exceptionally difficult, not only when it is straight ahead but also when coming from the side, flickering through a row of tree trunks.   In these circumstances a pair of sunglasses with wide, lateral 'blinkers' can be invaluable.

Never overlook the fact that when that low sun is behind you it will be blinding the drivers coming from the opposite direction.

The mindset of an advanced driver

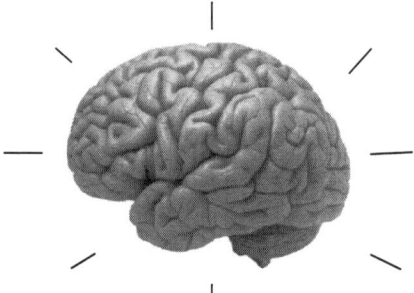

Perhaps this chapter should have been placed at the beginning but wherever it is placed it should form the dominant theme of your driving. Perhaps your mindset has changed for the better whilst you have been reading and the fact that you have got as far as this is a good omen. Whatever applies to you I hope that your enthusiasm and motivation are currently at a high level and furthermore that they will continue thus *for the rest of your life!*   Without the right mindset any improvement will be difficult to achieve.

Habits are extremely difficult to change.
Change requires a lot of effort and perseverance.
Effort requires a lot of motivation.

A **proactive approach** is needed in several areas. It won't just happen!

1. Attitudes
- Ambition and determination to become the best driver you can be.
- Legal compliance.
- Patience
- Humility
- Attitudes to other road users.

Motoring regulations may be perceived as having shortcomings but they are the best system me have for maintaining safety on the roads. It should always be remembered that the temptation to 'interpret' them introduces not only the danger of an 'incident' but also the danger of penalties. Advanced drivers comply with the law which actually contributes to enjoyable motoring.

Success in sport is measured in terms of winning.
Sport is nearly always a competitive activity having an aggressive motivation to prove oneself or one's team to be superior to the opposition.
The outcome of a motor race doesn't need to be explained to anyone.
And <u>herein lies part of the problem where driving is concerned</u>.

It is probably true to say that;
- The majority of drivers on the roads have an exaggerated idea of their own driving competence.
- A proportion of them are keen to impress all and sundry with their perceived driving superiority.
- There is something about being behind the wheel of a car that has the ability to change personalities.
- Even the most modest and laid back drivers (you and me) sometimes respond to a perceived challenge with an aggressive reaction even if the response is only verbal.

It is essential to recognise and resist this tendency

Remember that other driver's mistakes are rarely deliberate or aimed at you personally.

Above all avoid any inclination towards 'competitive driving'.

2. Learning

Any professional will tell you that learning is a continuous process throughout life   <u>Top sportsmen nearly all employ coaches.</u>

Be aware that no one is perfect.
Everyone makes mistakes
To learn we must be able to admit errors without criticism.
Every mistake is a learning opportunity.

3. Practice

Any athlete will tell you that lack of practice equates with being out of form.   There's no difference with driving.   Human nature is inherently lazy and always tends towards the easiest option.

To maintain the highest standards, skills must be practiced constantly.

4. Concentration

I have already written at some length about the importance of concentration and I make no apology for revisiting the topic as I believe concentration to be the most important part of driving safety and lack of concentration to be a principle or contributory element in all road collisions.

As I said previously
'Driving without due care and attention is a criminal offence'
No one can claim to be free from guilt in this respect.

As we get older the tendency for the mind to wander seems to increase for a variety of reasons. The only way to counteract lack of concentration is by recognising its insidious presence and taking active steps to counteract it.

Please, if you are a passenger, keep the conversation to essentials and avoid chatter when traffic conditions are difficult.

On the other hand it may be important to help prevent the onset of tiredness in the driver. In either case passengers can play their part.

Drivers should not only avoid distractions but should take positive steps to maintain a high level of driving awareness at all times.

Reading the road and planning the immediate course should become continuous and constant.

There is a multiple variety of official road signs (and occasionally unofficial ones too). These are all there for our benefit but sadly all too often they are neither seen nor registered consciously.

Make a point of registering the meaning of every sign you see.

The simplest way to do this is to talk to yourself – out loud if you are on your own or silently if you have a passenger. Then add in other things that you see which might influence the drive.
Perhaps this will lead to a comment on its significance.
Do you remember we previously talked about **'observation links'**?
If you simply follow a sequence of thought (and maybe verbalise it) you will soon find that **reading the road** is an automatic process.
By adding in your intended reaction to what you see you will be **planning** and **anticipating.**

This simple thought process is known as commentary.
It can be silent or spoken out loud when appropriate

All a commentary involves is focused thinking and
putting your thoughts into words.

In my opinion it is the best way of improving concentration.

Appendix
Observation Links

In addition to promoting safer driving, observation links are a means of increasing driving enjoyment and sense of satisfaction

Observation	Indication
On country Rd. People at bus stop on offside of the road	Bus coming from opposite direction
Bus stopped on nearside	Dismounting passengers crossing
Parked car with occupants	Opening offside doors
Parked car with exhaust or brake lights	Car about to move off
Country Rd. Lone lamp standard	Road junction on opposite side of road.
Country Rd. Distant lamp cluster	Cross roads with island
Country Rd. Trees across horizon with gap	Road bends towards gap
Country Rd. Telegraph poles deviate	Road usually deviates in same direction
Country Rd. Village sign	Expect speed reduction sign.
Country Rd. 'Cows' sign	Expect slippery road
M-way. 2 HGVs in slow lane approaching hill	Anticipate overtake manoeuvre.
M-way junction	Vehicles joining from slip road.
Country Rd Horse manure on road	Expect horses
Country Rd Rubbish bins.	Expect Rubbish Collection Vehicle

Observation	Indication
Puddle	may conceal a pot-hole
Country Rd. Distant traffic movement to the sides	Road junction ahead
Service station or garden centre etc.	Expect vehicles emerging
Foreign number plate or signs	L- hand drive. Poor rear visibility
Car with luggage blocking rear window	Driver may not be used to using his wing mirrors
Closely spaced lamp standards	Speed limit 30 (unless otherwise stated)
Oncoming vehicles using headlights in daylight	Fog or other hazard ahead
Loose objects fallen from vehicle	Expect more loose objects
Movement of trees	High side-winds on exposed roads
Stationary ice-cream van	Children crossing road
Railway running beside road.	Road crossing railway at sharp angle.
Increase vibration through wheels	Decreased traction
Frost in shaded patches.	Decreased traction
Wet Leaves	Decreased traction
Bicycle approaching grid or pothole	Expect wobbles
At night. Headlights of other vehicles	Indicate route of road and junctions